MW00681533

The complete illustrated
field reference

Jerry A. Klinke

ACRA Publishing
2769 West Glenlord
Stevensville, Michigan 49127
(616) 429-6240

ISBN 1-888724-00-5

Acknowledgments

The author would like to express his sincere appreciation to the following:

The ANSI/ASME standards used within this publication were used with the permission of The American Society of Mechanical Engineers, United Engineering Center, 345 East 47th Street, New York, N.Y., 10017.

The material related to the safe use of wire rope slings was used with the permission of The Wire Rope Technical Board, P.O. Box 849, Stevensville, Maryland, 21666.

Special thanks to Kim, Kara, and Kevin for their tolerance with me while I was involved in writing this book.

First Printing, December 1995
Second Printing, June 1996

Printed in U.S.A.
by Batson Printing, Inc.
Benton Harbor, Michigan

Introduction

The **RIGGING HANDBOOK** is a clear, illustrated reference source for persons working in the construction, industrial maintenance, or related fields that involve rigging and hoisting operations. This handbook basically represents the working notebook of the author. It is based on material assembled by the author to assist him in the construction and repairs associated with power plant components over the past 20 years.

This handbook provides concise, simple answers to rigging situations that may otherwise appear complex in nature. The notes explain and illustrate some of the basic and complex problems associated with a wide variety of rigging situations. Both apprentices and journeymen will appreciate the simple layout and organization of this valuable reference.

Data, specifications, engineering information and drawings presented in this publication have been delineated in accordance with recognized professional principles and practices, and are for general information only. Suggested procedures should not, therefore, be used without first securing competent engineering advice for any given application.

Contents

The information contained in this publication was compiled from sources believed to be reliable. It should not be assumed that this material covers all regulations or standards used in the construction industry. The author and publisher cannot guarantee correctness or completeness and accept no responsibility in the use or misuse of this information.

WIRE ROPE & SLINGS

Wire Rope types

Wire Rope is made of steel wires laid together to form a strand. These strands are laid together to form a rope, usually around a central core of either fiber or wire.

Fiber Core

A fiber core is composed of a synthetic fiber such as polypropylene, or a natural fiber like jute or hemp.

Wire Core

IWRC is the abbreviation for independent wire rope core. This wire core, which is actually another strand, adds about 7% to the overall strength. This is the most common construction used today.

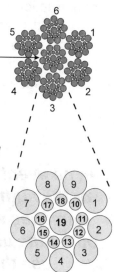

Independent Wire Rope Core (IWRC)

Strand Classification

Strands are grouped according to the number of wires per strand. This number defines a pattern, and is related to the typical strength of the wire rope. The first number indicates the number of strands in the rope, the second number indicates the number of wires within each strand. The number of wire is nominal and can vary, as shown in the table below.

Classification	Number of strands	Wires per strand
6 X 7	6	3 to 14
6 X 19	6	16 to 26
6 X 37	6	27 to 49
8 X 19	8	15 to 26

WRCLAS.TBL

Wire Rope Lay Length

The lay length of a wire rope is the straight linear distance of one strand as it makes a complete revolution.

Lay Length

Wire rope inspections.

The inspection criteria for wire rope depends entirely on the intended use, and the applicable regulatory code that the inspection is based on. The following table lists some of the more common standards that address inspection criteria.

ANSI Standard	Equipment
B30.2	Overhead & Gantry Cranes
B30.4	Portal, Tower & Pillar Cranes
B30.5	Crawler, Locomotive & Truck Cranes
B30.6	Derricks
B30.7	Base Mounted Drum Hoists
B30.8	Floating Cranes & Derricks
B30.16	Overhead Hoists
A10.4	Personnel Hoists
A10.5	Material Hoists

WR-ANSI.TBL

The manufacturer's recommendations should always be followed in determining the safe working loads of the various sizes and types of slings shown on the following pages. The tables contained within this book, are based on current ANSI, OSHA, and general industry standards. They are intended to assist the craftsman in the field, and are not intended to replace or supersede any manufacturers recommendations.

Strength of wire rope

SLINGS

6 X 19 and 6 X 37 Classification Improved Plow Steel, FIBER CORE, Wire rope				
Wire Rope Diameter	Breaking Strength lbs.	Breaking Strength tons	Safe Working Load -lbs	Safe Working Load - tons
3/16"	3,100	1.55	620	0.31
1/4"	5,480	2.74	1,096	0.55
5/16"	8,520	4.26	1,704	0.85
3/8"	12,200	6.10	2,440	1.22
7/16"	16,540	8.27	3,308	1.65
1/2"	21,400	10.70	4,280	2.14
9/16"	27,000	13.50	5,400	2.70
5/8"	33,400	16.70	6,680	3.34
3/4"	47,600	23.80	9,520	4.76
7/8"	64,400	32.20	12,880	6.44
1"	83,600	41.80	16,720	8.36
1-1/8"	105,200	52.60	21,040	10.52
1-1/4"	129,200	64.60	25,840	12.92
1-3/8"	155,400	77.70	31,080	15.54
1-1/2"	184,000	92.00	36,800	18.40
1-5/8"	214,000	107.00	42,800	21.40
1-3/4"	248,000	124.00	49,600	24.80
1-7/8"	282,000	141.00	56,400	28.20
2"	320,000	160.00	64,000	32.00

WR-S01.TBL

Wire Rope Diameter	Breaking Strength lbs.	Breaking Strength tons	Safe Working Load -lbs	Safe Working Load - tons
1/4"	6,800	3.40	1,360	0.68
5/16"	10,540	5.27	2,108	1.05
3/8"	15,100	7.55	3,020	1.51
7/16"	20,400	10.20	4,080	2.04
1/2"	26,600	13.30	5,320	2.66
9/16"	33,600	16.80	6,720	3.36
5/8"	41,200	20.60	8,240	4.12
3/4"	58,800	29.40	11,760	5.88
7/8"	79,600	39.80	15,920	7.96
1"	103,400	51.70	20,680	10.34
1-1/8"	130,000	65.00	26,000	13.00
1-1/4"	159,800	79.90	31,960	15.98
1-3/8"	192,000	96.00	38,400	19.20
1-1/2"	228,000	114.00	45,600	22.80
1-5/8"	264,000	132.00	52,800	26.40
1-3/4"	306,000	153.00	61,200	30.60
1-7/8"	348,000	174.00	69,600	34.80
2"	396,000	198.00	79,200	39.60

Table title: **6 X 19 and 6 X 37 Classification EXTRA Improved Plow Steel, I.W.R.C , Wire rope**

WR-S02.TBL

Uncoiling wire rope

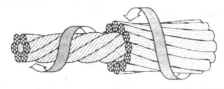

19 X 7 classification Rotation Resistant Wire Rope				
Wire Rope Diameter	Breaking Strength lbs.	Breaking Strength tons	Safe Working Load -lbs	Safe Working Load - tons
3/16"	2,840	1.42	284	0.14
1/4"	5,020	2.51	502	0.25
5/16"	7,800	3.9	780	0.39
3/8"	11,180	5.59	1,118	0.56
7/16"	15,160	7.58	1,516	0.76
1/2"	19,700	9.85	1,970	0.99
9/16"	24,800	12.40	2,480	1.24
5/8"	30,600	15.30	3,060	1.53
3/4"	43,600	21.80	4,360	2.18
7/8"	59,000	29.50	5,900	2.95
1"	76,600	38.30	7,660	3.83
1-1/8"	96,400	48.20	9,640	4.82

WR-S03.TBL

19 X 7 Strand Core Improved Plow Steel - Wires are preformed, commonly used in subways, sewers, and mines where a free load is suspended on a single line. The rotation resistant properties are achieved by fabricating the rope core and the outer strands with opposite twists.

Rotation may occur if the rope is too heavily loaded. To avoid this, these should be used with a design (safety) factor of 10:1, as shown above in the right hand columns.

Aircraft Cable

7 X 7 Aircraft Cable		
Wire Rope Diameter	Breaking Strength, in lbs.	
	Galvanized	304 Stainless Steel
1/16"	480	480
3/32"	920	920
1/8"	1,700	1,700
5/32"	2,600	2,400
3/16"	3,700	3,700

WR-S04.TBL

7 X 7 Strand Aircraft cable - Has high strength and rugged construction. Excellent for transmitting mechanical power. Commonly used for applications such as guying, control, and light hoisting or supporting.

7 X 19 Aircraft Cable		
Wire Rope Diameter	Breaking Strength, in lbs.	
	Galvanized	304 Stainless Steel
3/32"	1,000	920
1/8"	2,000	1,760
5/32"	2,800	2,400
3/16"	4,200	3,700
1/4"	7,000	6,400
5/16"	9,800	9,000
3/8"	14,400	12,000

WR-S05.TBL

7 X 19 Strand Aircraft cable - Has good strength and resistance to crushing loads. More flexible than the 7 X 7 construction. Commonly used for applications such as guying, control, and light hoisting or supporting.

Materials used in wire rope construction

STEEL

*Grade 130/140 and 120/130, Special
Improved Plow Type II
This is used when special installations require
maximum rope strength, such as mine shaft
hoisting.*

*Grade 110/120, Improved Plow Type I
This is most commonly used wire rope. It has
good wear resistance, high tensile strength,
and is fatigue resistant.*

*Grade 100/110 Plow
This rope has lower tensile but is used where
strength is secondary to wear resistance.*

STAINLESS STEEL

*Type 302 - High carbon content gives greater
strength, but less corrosion resistance.*

*Type 304 - medium carbon content, better
corrosion resistance.*

*Type 305 - Nonmagnetic, used around
electronic equipment and electromagnets.*

*Type 316 - Low carbon, good corrosion
resistance, used in marine applications.*

Wire Rope Slings

6 X 19 Classification, Improved Plow, I.W.R.C., Mechanical Splice			
Rope Size	Vertical	Choker	Basket
1/4"	1,120	840	2,200
5/16"	1,740	1,300	3,400
3/8"	2,400	1,860	5,000
7/16"	3,400	2,600	6,800
1/2"	4,400	3,200	8,800
9/16"	5,400	4,200	11,000
5/8"	6,800	5,000	13,600
3/4"	9,800	7,200	19,400
7/8"	13,200	9,800	26,000
1"	17,000	12,800	34,000
1-1/8"	20,000	15,600	42,000
6 X 37 Classification, Improved Plow, I.W.R.C., Mechanical Splice			
Rope Size	Vertical	Choker	Basket
1-1/4"	24,000	18,400	48,000
1-3/8"	30,000	22,000	58,000
1-1/2"	34,000	26,000	70,000
1-5/8"	40,000	30,000	82,000
1-3/4"	48,000	36,000	94,000
2"	60,000	46,000	122,000

WRICMS.TBL

SLINGS

6 X 19 Classification, Improved Plow, FIBER Core, Mechanical Splice			
Rope Size	**Vertical**	**Choker**	**Basket**
1/4"	1,020	760	2,000
5/16"	1,580	1,180	3,200
3/8"	2,200	1,700	4,400
7/16"	3,000	2,200	6,000
1/2"	4,000	3,000	7,800
9/16"	5,000	3,800	10,000
5/8"	6,200	4,600	12,400
3/4"	8,800	6,600	17,600
7/8"	11,800	9,000	24,000
1"	15,400	11,600	30,000
1-1/8"	19,000	14,200	38,000
6 X 37 Classification, Improved Plow, FIBER Core, Mechanical Splice			
Rope Size	**Vertical**	**Choker**	**Basket**
1-1/4"	22,000	16,600	44,000
1-3/8"	26,000	20,000	54,000
1-1/2"	32,000	24,000	64,000
1-5/8"	36,000	28,000	74,000
1-3/4"	42,000	32,000	86,000
2"	56,000	42,000	110,000

WRFCMS.TBL

6 X 19 Classification, Improved Plow, I.W.R.C., Hand Tucked			
Rope Size	**Vertical**	**Choker**	**Basket**
1/4"	1,060	800	2,000
5/16"	1,620	1,220	3,200
3/8"	2,200	1,720	4,600
7/16"	3,000	2,400	6,200
1/2"	4,000	3,000	7,800
9/16"	5,000	3,600	9,800
5/8"	6,000	4,400	12,000
3/4"	8,400	6,200	16,800
7/8"	11,000	8,200	22,000
1"	14,400	10,800	28,000
1-1/8"	18,000	13,600	36,000
6 X 37 Classification, Improved Plow, I.W.R.C., Hand Tucked			
Rope Size	**Vertical**	**Choker**	**Basket**
1-1/4"	20,000	15,800	42,000
1-3/8"	26,000	19,200	50,000
1-1/2"	30,000	22,000	60,000
1-5/8"	36,000	26,000	70,000
1-3/4"	40,000	30,000	82,000
2"	52,000	40,000	106,000

WRICHT.TBL

6 X 19 Classification, Improved Plow, FIBER Core, Hand Tucked			
Rope Size	**Vertical**	**Choker**	**Basket**
1/4"	980	740	1,980
5/16"	1,520	1,140	3,000
3/8"	2,200	1,600	4,200
7/16"	2,800	2,200	5,800
1/2"	3,600	2,800	7,400
9/16"	4,600	3,400	9,200
5/8"	5,600	4,200	11,200
3/4"	7,800	5,800	15,600
7/8"	10,200	7,800	20,000
1"	13,400	10,000	26,000
1-1/8"	16,800	12,600	34,000

6 X 37 Classification, Improved Plow, FIBER Core, Hand Tucked			
Rope Size	**Vertical**	**Choker**	**Basket**
1-1/4"	19,600	14,800	40,000
1-3/8"	24,000	17,800	48,000
1-1/2"	28,000	20,000	56,000
1-5/8"	32,000	24,000	66,000
1-3/4"	38,000	28,000	76,000
2"	50,000	36,000	98,000

WRFCHT.TBL

Roundslings

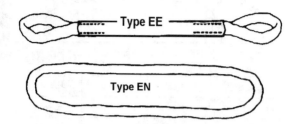

Synthetic RoundSlings Safe Working Limits (in lbs)			
Color	Vertical	Choker	Basket
PURPLE	2,650	2,120	5,300
GREEN	5,300	4,240	10,600
YELLOW	8,400	6,720	16,800
TAN	10,600	8,500	21,200
RED	13,200	10,560	26,400
ORANGE	16,800	13,440	33,600
BLUE	21,200	17,000	42,400
GREY	31,700	25,300	63,400
BROWN	52,900	42,300	105,800
OLIVE	66,100	52,880	132,200
BLACK	90,000	72,000	180,000

RS-SWL.TBL

Basic Sling Types

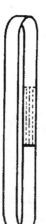

Type 5, EN Slings - Endless slings, sometimes also referred to as grommet slings. A very common sling used in most applications.

Type 3 (left) and Type 4 (right) are both identified as EE Slings - Both ends have an eye formed by stitching the material in the middle together. Type 4 has a twisted eye, but otherwise is identical to the Type 3.

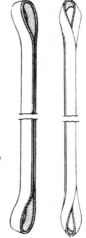

1 ply	Synthetic NYLON web slings, Single ply construction - type EE Safe Working Limits (in lbs)		
Width	Vertical	Choker	Basket
1"	1,600	1,200	3,200
2"	3,200	2,400	6,400
3"	4,800	3,600	9,600
4"	6,400	4,800	12,800
5"	8,000	6,000	16,000
6"	9,600	7,200	19,200

NSE1-SWL.TBL

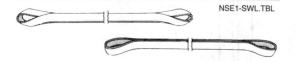

2 ply	Synthetic NYLON web slings, Two-ply construction - type EE Safe Working Limits (in lbs)		
Width	Vertical	Choker	Basket
1"	3,200	2,400	6,400
2"	6,400	4,800	12,800
3"	8,600	6,500	17,200
4"	11,500	8,600	23,000
5"	13,600	10,200	27,200
6"	16,300	12,200	32,600
8"	19,200	15,400	38,400
10"	22,400	17,900	44,800
12"	26,900	21,500	53,800

NSE2-SWL.TBL

Nylon Web slings

1 ply	Synthetic NYLON web slings, Single ply construction - type EN Safe Working Limits (in lbs)		
Width	Vertical	Choker	Basket
1"	3,200	2,500	6,400
2"	6,400	5,000	12,800
3"	8,600	6,900	17,200
4"	11,500	9,200	23,000
5"	13,600	10,900	27,200
6"	16,300	13,000	32,600

NSN1-SWL.TBL

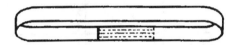

2 ply	Synthetic NYLON web slings, Two ply construction - type EN Safe Working Limits (in lbs)		
Width	Vertical	Choker	Basket
1"	6,100	4,900	12,200
2"	12,200	9,800	24,400
3"	16,300	13,000	32,600
4"	20,700	16,500	41,400
5"	24,500	19,600	49,000
6"	28,600	23,000	57,200

NSN2-SWL.TBL

Wire Mesh Slings

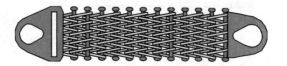

Metal Mesh, HEAVY DUTY
10 Ga., #35
Rated Capacities (in lbs)

Sling Width (in inches)	Vertical or Choker	Vertical Basket
2	1,500	3,000
3	2,700	5,400
4	4,000	8,000
6	6,000	12,000
8	8,000	16,000
10	10,000	20,000
12	12,000	24,000
14	14,000	28,000
16	16,000	32,000
18	18,000	36,000
20	20,000	40,000

MMHD35.TBL

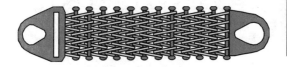

Metal Mesh, MEDIUM DUTY
12 Ga., #43
Rated Capacities (in lbs)

Sling Width (in inches)	Vertical or Choker	Vertical Basket
2	1,350	2,700
3	2,000	4,000
4	2,700	5,400
6	4,500	9,000
8	6,000	12,000
10	7,500	15,000
12	9,000	18,000
14	10,500	21,000
16	12,000	24,000
18	13,500	27,000
20	1,500	30,000

MMMD43.TBL

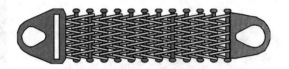

Metal Mesh, LIGHT DUTY 14 Ga., #59 Rated Capacities (in lbs)		
Sling Width (in inches)	Vertical or Choker	Vertical Basket
2	900	1,800
3	1,400	2,800
4	2,000	4,000
6	3,000	6,000
8	4,000	8,000
10	5,000	10,000
12	6,000	12,000
14	7,000	14,000
16	8,000	16,000
18	9,000	18,000
20	10,000	20,000

MMLD59.TBL

Alloy Chain Slings

\multicolumn{2}{c}{Rated Capacity for Alloy Steel Chain Slings (in lbs)}	
Chain Size	**Single Vertical**
1/4"	3,250
3/8"	6,600
1/2"	11,250
5/8"	16,500
3/4"	23,000
7/8"	28,750
1"	38,750
1-1/8"	44,500
1-1/4"	57,500
1-3/8"	67,000

CS-001.TBL

When chain slings, or any other type of sling, is used at an angle other than vertical the safe working load (SWL) is always reduced. The following tables list the reduced SWL at a given angle. These ratings are based on ANSI B30.9, consult the manufacturers rating for specific chains and equipment. NEVER EXCEED THE SAFE WORKING LIMIT!

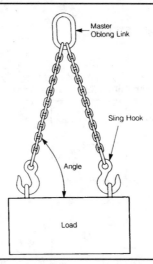

Double Chain (Alloy) Slings Rated Capacity, in lbs			
Chain Size	60 degrees	45 degrees	30 degrees
1/4"	5,650	4,550	3,250
3/8"	11,400	9,300	6,600
1/2"	19,500	15,900	11,250
5/8"	28,500	23,300	16,500
3/4"	39,800	32,500	23,000
7/8"	49,800	40,600	28,750
1"	67,100	54,800	38,750
1-1/8"	77,000	63,000	44,500
1-1/4"	99,500	81,000	57,500
1-3/8"	116,000	94,000	67,000
1-1/2"	138,000	112,500	80,000

CS-002.TBL

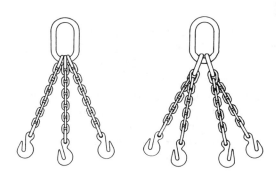

Triple & Quadruple Chain (Alloy) Slings Rated Capacity, in lbs			
Chain Size	60 degrees	45 degrees	30 degrees
1/4"	8,400	6,800	4,900
3/8"	17,000	14,000	9,900
1/2"	29,000	24,000	17,000
5/8"	43,000	35,000	24,500
3/4"	59,500	48,500	34,500
7/8"	74,500	61,000	43,000
1"	101,000	82,000	58,000
1-1/8"	115,500	94,500	66,500
1-1/4"	149,000	121,500	86,000
1-3/8"	174,000	141,000	100,500
1-1/2"	207,000	169,000	119,500

CS-003.TBL

HARDWARE

The hardware, or tackle used with rigging installations is just as important as the slings and wire ropes used. Just as with slings, the angular rigging situations place additional stresses on these components as well. All hardware is rated as if straight, linear tension is applied. The Safe Working Load (S.W.L.) ratings are reduced drastically when equipment is used improperly, or at angles other than designed for.

Eyebolts are one of the most abused rigging hardware components, these generally fail when angular loads are applied incorrectly for the situation.

It is recommended that all eye bolts used for hoisting be made from forged alloy steel and equipped with shoulders. The plain or shoulderless eye bolt is acceptable for vertical loading, but when subjected to angular loading it will bend or break.

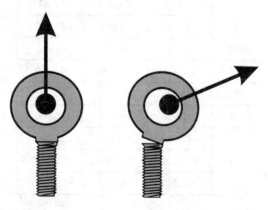

Even when using shouldered eye bolts, the safe working load MUST be decreased as shown in the tables on the following pages.

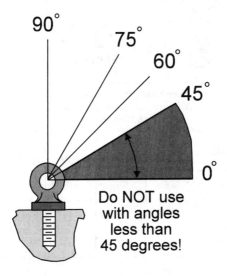

Do NOT use with angles less than 45 degrees!

The best choice for angular loading is to use a hoist ring, sometimes called a "swivel eye bolt". These have the same SWL regardless of the angle used.

Eye Bolts, Shoulder

These values can also be used with properly installed eye nuts .

Eye Bolts, Machinery type with shoulder (forged steel) rated SWL in lbs				
SIZE	45 degree	60 degree	75 degree	90 degree
1/4"	125	175	275	500
5/16"	200	280	440	800
3/8"	300	420	680	1,200
1/2"	550	770	1,210	2,200
5/8"	875	1,225	1,925	3,500
3/4"	1,300	1,820	2,860	5,200
7/8"	1,800	2,520	3,960	7,200
1"	2,500	3,500	5,500	10,000
1-1/4"	3,800	5,320	8,360	15,200
1-1/2"	5,350	7,490	11,770	21,400

EYE-M.TBL

Eye bolt alignment

Where shouldered eye bolts cannot be kept in line with each other, and maintain securely tightened, shims must be inserted under the shoulder to permit alignment. Then following table lists the shim details to maintain alignment.

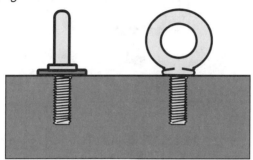

Eye Bolt size (inches)	Shim Thickness Required to change rotation 90 degrees (inches)
1/4" X 20 TPI	0.0125
5/16" X 18 TPI	0.0139
3/8" X 16 TPI	0.0156
1/2" X 13 TPI	0.0192
5/8" X 11 TPI	0.0227
3/4" X 10 TPI	0.025
7/8" X 9 TPI	0.0278
1" X 8 TPI	0.0312
1-1/4" X 7 TPI	0.0357
1-1/2" C 6 TPI	0.0417

EYESHIM.TBL

Hoist Rings

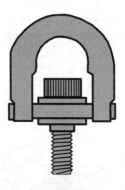

Hoist Rings		
Thread Size	**SWL in pounds**	**Torque (lb. ft.)**
5/16"	800	7
3/8"	1,000	12
1/2"	2,500	28
5/8"	4,000	60
3/4"	7,000	100
7/8"	8,000	160
1"	10,000	230
1-1/4"	15,000	470
1-1/2"	24,000	800
2"	30,000	800

EYE-HR.TBL

Side-pull Hoist Rings

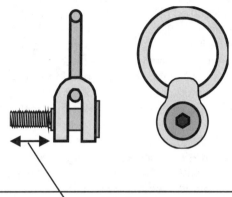

HARDWARE

	Side-Pull Hoist Rings		
Thread Size	Minimum Thread Engagement	SWL in pounds	Torque (lb. ft.)
5/16"	5/8"	650	3.50
3/8"	3/4"	800	4.50
1/2"	1"	1,800	15.00
5/8"	1-1/4"	2,500	25
3/4"	1-1/2"	4,100	50
1"	2"	7,100	90
1-1/4"	2"	14,000	150
1-1/2"	2-1/2"	17,200	250
2"	3-1/8"	29,000	300

EYE-HRS.TBL

The most common method used to make an eye or attach a wire rope to a piece of equipment is with a cable or Crosby clip. When installed properly these will develop approximately 80% of the rope strength, however if improperly installed they can reduce the efficiency of the connection to 40%. It is also important to have the proper spacing and number of clips, the tables on the following pages list the most common installations. The proper torque on the bolts is important also, this ensures that the threads are not over stressed or under tightened.

The cartoon below depicts a common phrase that is used throughout the industry to help people remember the correct way to install Crosby wire rope clips.

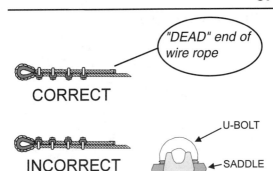

CORRECT

INCORRECT

U-BOLT

SADDLE

STEP 1

Refer to the table on the next page to obtain the turn back space. Apply first clip one base width from the dead end of the rope. Tighten nuts evenly and torque per the recommended value.

STEP 2

Apply the second clip as near to the loop as possible. Tighten nuts evenly and torque per the recommended value.

STEP 3

Apply the rest of the clips as indicated in the tables. Space clips accordingly and torque.

Crosby wire rope clip

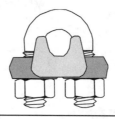

(Crosby) Wire Rope Clips - Installation data				
Rope Diameter	**No. of Clips**	**Turnback**	**Spacing**	**Torque in Foot-lbs (unlubed bolts)**
1/8"	2	3-1/4"	3/4"	-
3/16"	2	3-3/4"	1-1/8"	-
1/4"	2	4-3/4"	1-1/2"	15
5/16"	2	5-1/2"	1-7/8"	30
3/8"	2	6-1/2"	2-1/4"	45
7/16"	2	7"	2-5/8"	65
1/2"	3	11-1/2"	3"	65
9/16"	3	12"	3-3/8"	95
5/8"	3	12"	3-3/4"	95
3/4"	4	18"	4-1/2"	130
7/8"	4	19"	5-1/4"	225
1"	5	26"	6"	225
1-1/8"	6	34"	6-3/4"	225
1-1/4"	6	37"	7-1/2"	360
1-3/8"	7	44"	8-1/4"	360
1-1/2"	7	48"	9"	360
1-5/8"	7	51"	9-3/4"	430
1-3/4"	7	53"	10-1/2"	590
2"	8	71"	12"	750
2-1/4"	8	73"	13-1/2"	750

CROS-R.TBL

Double saddle clips

These are preferable to the Crosby type because of the ease of installation. Correctly installed they will have minimal damage to the wire rope as compared to the saddle and u-bolt types.

HARDWARE

Double Saddle, Wire Rope Clips - Installation data				
Rope Diameter	No. of Clips	Turnback	Spacing	Torque in Foot-lbs (unlubed bolts)
3/16"	2	4"	1-1/8"	30
1/4"	2	4"	1-1/2"	30
5/16"	2	5"	1-7/8"	30
3/8"	2	5-1/2"	2-1/4"	45
7/16"	2	6-1/2"	2-5/8"	65
1/2"	3	11"	3"	65
9/16"	3	12-3/4"	3-3/8"	130
5/8"	3	13-1/2"	3-3/4"	130
3/4"	3	16"	4-1/2"	225
7/8"	4	26"	5-1/4"	225
1"	5	37"	6"	225
1-1/8"	5	41"	6-3/4"	360
1-1/4"	6	55"	7-1/2"	360
1-3/8"	6	62"	8-1/4"	500
1-1/2"	6	66"	9"	500

CROS-D.TBL

Shackles

Shackle sizes are based on the size of the bow ("C"), not the bolt or thread size.

Typical Shackle Dimensions (in inches)			
SIZE	A	B	C
3/16"	0.380	0.250	0.190
1/4"	0.470	0.310	0.250
5/16"	0.530	0.380	0.310
3/8"	0.660	0.440	0.380
7/16"	0.750	0.500	0.440
1/2"	0.810	0.630	0.500
5/8"	1.060	0.750	0.690
3/4"	1.250	0.880	0.810
7/8"	1.440	1.000	0.970
1"	1.690	1.130	1.060
1-1/8"	1.810	1.250	1.250
1-1/4"	2.030	1.380	1.380
1-3/8"	2.250	1.500	1.500
1-1/2"	2.380	1.630	1.620
1-3/4"	2.880	2.000	2.250
2"	3.250	2.250	2.400
2-1/2"	4.130	2.750	3.130
3"	5.000	3.250	3.620
3-1/2"	5.750	3.750	4.120
4"	6.500	4.250	4.560

SHKSIZE.TBL

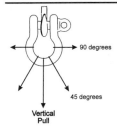

Angular reduction is based on load weight, not leg tension.

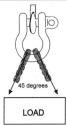

LOAD

Shackles Safe Working Load			
Size	Vertical Pull	45 Degrees	90 degrees
3/16"	655	459	328
1/4"	1,000	700	500
5/16"	1,500	1,050	750
3/8"	2,000	1,400	1,000
7/16"	3,000	2,100	1,500
1/2"	4,000	2,800	2,000
5/8"	6,500	4,550	3,250
3/4"	9,500	6,650	4,750
7/8"	13,000	9,100	6,500
1"	17,000	11,900	8,500
1-1/8"	19,000	13,300	9,500
1-1/4"	24,000	16,800	12,000
1-3/8"	27,000	18,900	13,500
1-1/2"	34,000	23,800	17,000
1-3/4"	50,000	35,000	25,000
2"	70,000	49,000	35,000
2-1/2"	100,000	70,000	50,000
3"	150,000	105,000	75,000
3-1/2"	200,000	140,000	100,000
4"	260,000	182,000	130,000

HARDWARE

SHK-SWL.TBL

Sliding Choker Hooks Forged alloy steel		
Throat Opening (inches)	**Rope Size (inches)**	**Maximum Safe Working Load (lbs)**
1/2"	1/4"	1,500
5/8"	3/8"	2,600
7/8"	1/2"	3,400
1"	5/8"	5,100
1-1/8"	3/4"	8,000

HOOK-1.TBL

Sliding choker hooks

Chain Slip Hooks   Chain GRAB Hooks

HARDWARE

SLIP HOOKS Throat Opening (inches)	GRAB HOOKS Throat Opening (inches)	Chain Hooks	
		Chain Size (inches)	Maximum Safe Working Load (lbs)
15/16"	11/32"	1/4"	2,750
1-1/16"	7/16"	5/16"	4,300
1-5/16"	1/2"	3/8"	5,250
1-9/16"	9/16"	7/16"	7,000
1-11/16"	21/32"	1/2"	9,000
2"	25/32"	5/8"	13,500
2-1/8"	15/16"	3/4"	19,250
2-3/4"	1-1/16"	7/8"	26,000
3"	1-3/16"	1"	34,000

HOOK-2.TBL

Chain Hooks

RINGS

Stock Diameter (inches)	Inside Diameter (inches)	Maximum Safe Working Load (lbs)
7/8"	4"	7,200
7/8"	5-1/2"	5,600
1"	4"	10,800
1-1/8"	6"	10,400
1-1/4"	5"	17,000
1-3/8"	6"	19,000

RING.TBL

PEAR SHAPED LINKS

Stock Diameter (inches)	Inside Length (inches)	Maximum Safe Working Load (lbs)
3/8"	2-1/4"	1,800
1/2"	3"	2,900
5/8"	3-3/4"	4,200
3/4"	4-1/2"	6,000
7/8"	5-1/4"	8,300
1"	6"	10,800
1-1/4"	7-3/4"	16,750
1-3/8"	8-1/4"	20,500

PEAR.TBL

MASTER LINKS

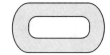

Stock Diameter (inches)	Inside Width (inches)	Maximum Safe Working Load (lbs)
1/2"	2-1/2"	3,250
5/8"	3"	4,400
3/4"	2-3/4"	7,000
1"	3-1/2"	16,500
1-1/4"	4-3/8"	25,000
1-1/2"	5-1/4"	35,500
1-3/4"	6"	44,500
2"	7"	57,500

MASTER.TBL

HARDWARE

TWIN CLEVIS LINK

Chain Size (inches)	Maximum Safe Working Load (lbs)
1/4" - 5/16"	4,700
3/8"	6,600
7/16" - 1/2"	11,250

T-CLEVIS.TBL

DOUBLE CLEVIS LINK

Chain Size (inches)	Maximum Safe Working Load (lbs)
1/4"	2,600
5/16" - 3/8"	5,400
7/16"	7,000
1/2"	9,200

D-CLEVIS.TBL

Swivels

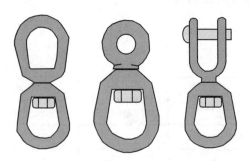

SWIVELS (all types)

Stock Diameter (inches)	Maximum Safe Working Load (lbs)
1/4"	850
5/16"	1,250
3/8"	2,250
1/2"	3,600
5/8"	5,200
3/4"	7,200
7/8"	10,000
1"	12,500
1-1/8"	15,200
1-1/4"	18,000
1-1/2"	45,200

SWIVELS.TBL

Turnbuckles

Jaw and Eye Combination

Jaw and Jaw Combination

Hook and Hook Combination

Hook and Eye Combination

HARDWARE

Thread Diameter	Safe Working Load (in lbs)	
	EYE & JAW end fitting types	HOOK end fitting type
1/4"	500	400
5/16"	800	700
3/8"	1,200	1,000
1/2"	2,200	1,500
5/8"	3,500	2,250
3/4"	5,200	3,000
7/8"	7,200	4,000
1"	10,000	5,000
1-1/4"	15,200	5,000
1-1/2"	21,400	7,500

TURNBKL.TBL

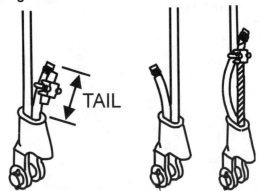

Wire Rope Diameter	Standard, 6 to 8 strand wire rope	Rotation Resistant wire rope *
	MINIMUM TAIL LENGTH	
1/4" to 1"	6"	20"
1" to 1-3/8"	8-1/4"	27-1/2"
1-1/2" to 1-7/8"	11-1/4"	37-1/2"
2" to 2-3/4"	16-1/2"	55"

WEDGE.TBL

* Rotation Resistant Rope: Special wire rope constructions with 8 or more outer strands. Ensure that the dead end is brazed or seized before inserting into the wedge socket to prevent core slippage (see page 13).

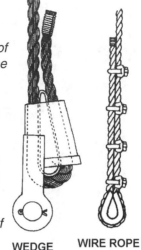

End attachment strength

End attachments of wire rope are of the greatest importance to safety. Many wire rope attachments develop less than full strength of the wire rope. Always consult the manufacturer for the exact values of the equipment. These examples are based on typical equipment and installations.

HARDWARE

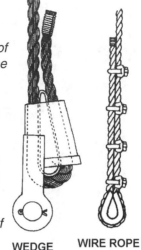

WEDGE

WIRE ROPE with thimble

80%

FLEMISH EYE with mechanical pressed sleeve

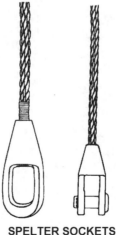

SPELTER SOCKETS

100%

MATH

A lift cannot be safely made until all involved parties agree that the crane and rigging are operating within their capacity. The crane operator and the rigger must be told the exact weight of the load, or determine the weight for themselves.

To determine weight, use all available information such as drawings, shipping bills, parts manuals, etc.

If none of these are available, the rigger must estimate the weight based on volume.

The following pages show some basic shapes and the formulas related to determining the volume of the object.

Remember, when in doubt OVER estimate! It's better to over rig than under rig......

Weight of materials

The basic formula to determine the weight of an object is:

WEIGHT=VOLUME X WEIGHT OF MATERIAL

Standard weights of typical materials		
Material	**Cu. ft**	**Cu. Inch**
Aluminum	165.00	0.0955
Brass	535.00	0.3096
Brick masonry, common	125.00	0.0723
Bronze	500.00	0.2894
Cast Iron	480.00	0.2778
Cement, portland, loose	94.00	0.0544
Concrete, stone aggr.	144.00	0.0833
Copper	560.00	0.3241
Earth, dry	75.00	0.0434
Earth, wet	100.00	0.0579
Glass	160.00	0.0926
Ice	56.00	0.0324
Lead	710.00	0.4109
Snow, fresh fallen	8.00	0.0046
Snow, wet	35.00	0.0203
Steel	490.00	0.2836
Tin	460.00	0.2662
Water	62.00	0.0359
Gypsum wall board	54.00	0.0313
Wood, pine	30.00	0.0174

(Values listed are in U.S. pounds)   WEIGHT.TBL

Cube or rectangle.

1.) Determine the volume of the object.
   a X b X c = Volume

2.) Determine the Approximate weight of the object.
   Volume X Weight (per Cu)

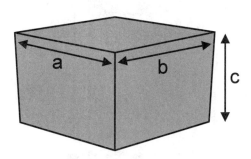

MATH

EXAMPLE:
a=12 inches   b=24inches   c=5 inches
Material=Steel

Step one, find the volume:
12 X 24 X 5 = 1440 Cu inches

Step two, find weight:
1440 X .2836 = **408.38 lb**

Round Shapes

1.) Determine the volume of the object.
VOLUME = 0.7854 X D X D X H

2.) Determine the Approximate weight of the
  object.
WEIGHT = Volume X Weight (per Cu)

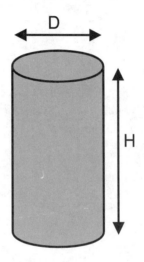

EXAMPLE:
D=18 inches   H=42inches
Material=Steel

Step one, find the volume:
0.7854 X 18 X 18 X 42 = 10687.72 Cu inches

Step two, find weight:
10687.72 X .2836 = **3031.03 lbs**

Round & Hollow (Pipe)

1.)Determine the volume of the object.
VOLUME = T X (D-T) X 3.141 X H

2.)Determine the Approximate weight of the
object.
WEIGHT = Volume X Weight (per Cu)

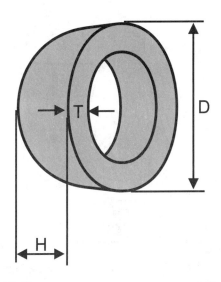

MATH

EXAMPLE:
D=18 inches   T=1.5 inches   H=48 inches
Material=Steel

Step one, find the volume:
1.5 X (18-1.5) X 3.141 X 48 = 3731.5 Cu in

Step two, find weight:
3731.5 X .2836 = **1058.25 lbs**

Fustum of a cone

1.)Determine the volume of the object.
VOLUME = 0.2618 X h X (D^2 + Dxd + d^2)

2.)Determine the Approximate weight of the object.
WEIGHT = Volume X Weight (per Cu)

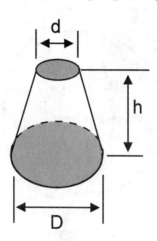

EXAMPLE:
d=6 inches   D=18 inches   h=32 inches
Material=Steel

Step one, find the volume:
0.2618 X 32 X ((18X18)+(18X6)+(6X6))=
3920.71 Cu inches
                or...
0.2618 X 32 X (468) = 3920.71 Cu inches

Step two, find weight:
3920.71 X .2836 = **1111.91 lbs**

The four shapes covered on the previous pages will allow you to determine the approximate weight of almost any object. For example examine the illustration of a valve bonnet below, notice that if you visualize it as separate shapes you can easily determine its approximate weight.

When in doubt, estimate on the HIGH side. It is always better to OVER RIG than UNDER RIG.

The following applies to the illustration of the valve bonnet shown below.

1.) Is considered round & hollow.
2.) Is a fustum of a cone.
3.) Is the hole in the center.
(figure the hole as a solid round shape, then subtract its weight from the fustum.)
4.) Is considered round & hollow.

MATH

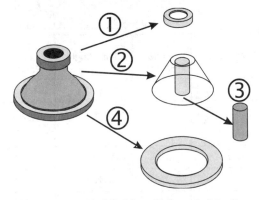

Remember, establishing the weight of an object is one of the most important steps in determining what type of rigging equipment to use for a safe lift!

Sling leg stress - angle method

To determine the amount of tension on a sling used at angles other that 90 degrees (vertical) use the following formula:

(Weight ÷ No of legs) x Load angle Factor

Example: If the load weight is 4,000 lbs, and two (2) slings are used at a 40 degree angle each.

(4000 ÷2) x 1.555
or
2000 x 1.555 = 3,110

Therefore, each leg will carry 3,110 lbs of tension.

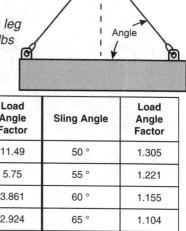

Angle

Sling Angle	Load Angle Factor	Sling Angle	Load Angle Factor
5 °	11.49	50 °	1.305
10 °	5.75	55 °	1.221
15 °	3.861	60 °	1.155
20 °	2.924	65 °	1.104
25 °	2.364	70 °	1.064
30 °	2.00	75 °	1.035
35 °	1.742	80 °	1.015
40 °	1.555	85 °	1.004
45 °	1.414	90 °	1.00

STRESS.TBL

Sling leg stress - field method

It is hard to determine the exact angle when working in the field, the following formula provides accurate calculations by using only measurements taken in the field:

(Weight ÷ No of legs) X (S ÷ H)

Example: If the load weight is 4,000 lbs, and two (2) slings are used that are 12 feet (144 inches) long, and the height from the load to the hook is 92-1/2".

(4000 ÷ 2) x (144 ÷ 92.5)
or
2000   x   1.556   = 3,112

Therefore, each leg will carry 3,112 lbs of tension. In addition, you can use this "load factor" number with the chart on the left and determine the approximate angle.

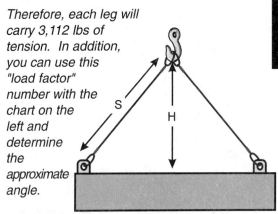

MATH

CAUTION:
These formulas are for any number of sling legs, but it is strongly recommended that the formula be used for two legs, as there is no way to assure that each leg will carry its share of the load. It is possible to have all the weight on two legs even with a four leg bridle due to load imbalance, or different leg lengths.

Drifting Loads

To determine how much tension will be placed upon chainfalls used in angular rigging situations, use the following formula:

Tension on Chainfall "A"
(Load × D2 × LA) ÷ (H × D3) = A

Tension on Chainfall "B"
(Load × D1 × LB) ÷ (H × D3) = B

NOTE: This formula is based on both chainfalls positioned at the same elevation.

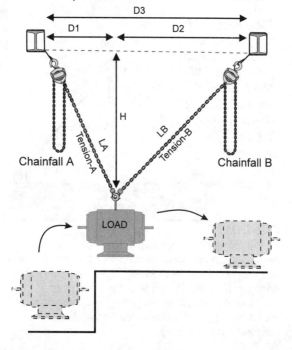

EXAMPLE:
D1 = 48"   D2 = 96"   D3 = 144"
LA = 60"   LB = 102.5"   H = 36"
Weight of load= 2,000 lbs

Chainfall "A"
(Load × D2 × LA) ÷ (H × D3) = A

(Load × D2 × LA)
2000 x 96 x 60 = 11,520,000

> **(H × D3)**
> *36 x 144 = 5,184*

11,520,000 ÷ 5,184 = 2,222 lbs tension

● ●

Chainfall "B"
(Load × D1 × LB) ÷ (H × D3) = B

(Load × D1 × LB)
2000 x 48 x 102.5 = 9,840,000

> **(H × D3)**
> *36 x 144 = 5,184*

9,840,000 ÷ 5,184 = 1,898 lbs tension

MATH

Sling Tightlines

To determine how much tension will be placed upon slings used in angular rigging situations, use the following formula:

Tension on the Left Sling (LS)
(Load × D2 × LS) ÷ (H × D3) = Tension- LS

Tension on the Right Sling (RS)
(Load × D1 × RS) ÷ (H × D3) = Tension-RS

NOTE: This formula is based on both slings attached at the same elevation.

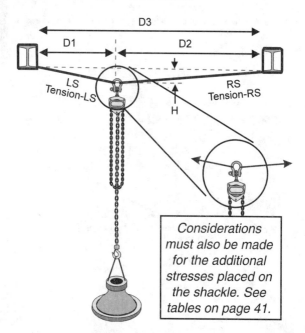

Considerations must also be made for the additional stresses placed on the shackle. See tables on page 41.

EXAMPLE:
D1 = 40"   D2 = 105"   D3 = 145"
LS = 48"   RS = 120"   H = 28"
Weight of load= 1,000 lbs

Tension on LEFT Sling:
(Load × D2 × LS) ÷ (H × D3)

(Load × D2 × LS)
1000 x 105 x 48 = 5,040,000

               (H × D3)
               28 x 145 = 4,060

5,040,000 ÷ 4,060 = 1,241 lbs tension

• •

Tension on RIGHT Sling:
(Load × D1 × RS) ÷ (H × D3)

(Load × D1 × RS)
1000 x 40 x 120 = 4,800,000

               (H × D3)
               28 x 145 = 4,060

4,800,000 ÷ 4,060 = 1,182 lbs tension

MATH

Figure A

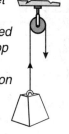

The mechanical advantage of a set of pulleys is the amount by which the pulleys multiply the force applied to it in order to lift the load. The top fixed pulley will have no other function than to change the direction of the rope. The lower, traveling block will create a mechanical advantage of 2:1 on each pulley.

Calculating mechanical advantage

Count the number of lines supporting the load, with the exception of the lead line when it comes down from the top pulley. If the lead lines comes up from the lower block (see figure D), then it can be counted as a supporting line and included in the mechanical advantage.

Figure A - *The mechanical advantage is 1:1. Assuming that the load is 1000 lbs, the amount of force required to lift the load would be 1000 lbs (1000 ÷ 1 = 1000).*

Figure B

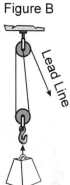

Figure B - *The mechanical advantage is 2:1. Assuming that the load is 1000 lbs, the amount of force required to lift the load would be 500 lbs (1000 ÷ 2 = 500).*

Figure C - The mechanical advantage is 4:1. Assuming that the load is 1000 lbs, the amount of force required to lift the load would be 250 lbs (1000 ÷ 4 = 250).

Figure D - The mechanical advantage is 5:1. Since the lead line is coming from the movable block, this line will be considered as part of the mechanical advantage. Assuming that the load is 1000 lbs, the amount of force required to lift the load would be 200 lbs (1000 ÷ 5 = 200).

Figure C   Figure D

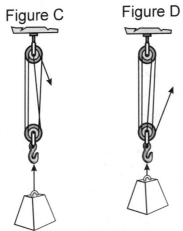

Block and line travel distance.

The distance the lead line will travel to lift the load is calculated by dividing the parts of line between the movable and stationary blocks and the distance the load is to be lifted. For example, using figure C and lifting the load 1 foot will require the lead line to travel 4 feet [4 (lines) ÷ 1 (foot) = 4 (feet)].

MATH

Block & Fairlead Loading

A single sheave block used to change load line direction can be subjected to total loads greatly different from the weight being lifted or pulled. The total load value varies with the angle between the incoming and departing lines to the block.

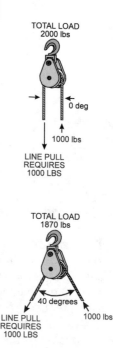

Multiplcation Factors for snatch blocks	
Angle	**Multiplication Factor**
0 °	2.00
10 °	1.99
20 °	1.97
30 °	1.93
40 °	1.87
50 °	1.81
60 °	1.73
70 °	1.64
80 °	1.53
90 °	1.41
100 °	1.29
110 °	1.15
120 °	1.00
130 °	0.84
140 °	0.68
150 °	0.52
160 °	0.35
170 °	0.17
180 °	0.00

SNBLK-01.TBL

EXAMPLE:
Since the block "A" is a traveling block, the
mechanical advantage is 2 because two parts
of load line support the 1,000 lbs load.*

To determine line pull:
1000 ÷ 2 = 500 lbs

To determine load on block "A":
500 lbs × 2.00 = 1,000 lbs
(line pull) × (factor of 0 degrees)

To determine load on block "B":
500 lbs × 1.87 + 500 lbs = 1,435 lbs

To determine load on block "C":
500 lbs × .84 = 420 lbs

To determine load on block "D":
500 lbs × 1.41 = 705 lbs

MATH

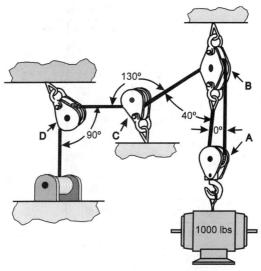

* *Block bearing friction NOT considered*

Level & Incline Planes

FORMULAS

LEVEL	**CF x W = F**
UPHILL	**(CF x W) + [(H ÷ R) x W] = F**
DOWNHILL	**(CF x W) - [(H ÷ R) x W] = F**

LEGEND	
W =	Weight of load (gross)
CF =	Coefficient of friction
F =	Force required to move load
H =	Height in feet
R =	RUN (Horizontal distance in feet)

COEF-LG.TBL

Coefficients of Friction		
Material	**Clean/Dry**	**Lubricated**
Concrete on concrete	0.65	0.15
Metal on concrete	0.60	0.15
Steel on steel	0.8	0.15
Cast iron on steel	0.4	0.21
Load on wheels	0.05	-----
Load on ice	0.01	-----
Load on cusion of air	0.002	-----
Wood on wood	0.45	0.3
Wood on metal	0.55	0.25
Wood on concrete	0.45	0.22

COEFF.TBL

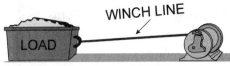

To move a load on a LEVEL plane
CF x W = F

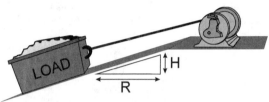

To move a load on an UPHILL incline
(CF x W) + [(H ÷ R) x W] = F

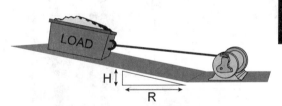

To move a load on a DOWNHILL plane
(CF x W) - [(H ÷ R) x W] = F

EXAMPLE:
The load weighs 10,000 lbs, and is steel on a dry concrete UPHILL incline. The "H' dimension is 5 ft., the "R" dimension is 9 ft.

(.60 x 10000) + [(.555) x 10000] = 11,555 lbs force
            or
(6,000) + [5,550] = 11,555 lbs of force

MATH

Non-Symmetrical Bridle Sling Formula

Calculating the stress on non-symmetrical bridle hitches is more complex that the normal sling formula. Because of the imbalance of load weight, you must determine the center of gravity first. Then the sling tensions can be determined using the formulas listed below.

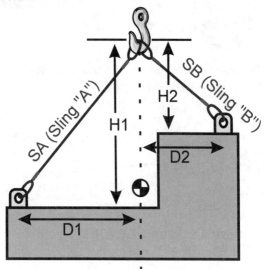

FORMULAS

Sling "A" Tension
(Load x D2 x SA) ÷ [(D2 x H1) + (D1 x H2)]

Sling "B" Tension
(Load x D1 x SB) ÷ [(D2 x H1) + (D1 x H2)]

EXAMPLE:
D1 = 55"   D2 = 27"   H1 = 60"
SA = 81"   SB = 30"   H2 = 24"
Weight of load= 6,000 lbs

Tension on Sling "A":
(Load × D2 × SA) ÷ [(D2 × H1) + (D1 × H2)]

(Load × D2 × SA)
6000 x 27 x 81 = 13,122,000

(D2 × H1) + (D1 × H2)
(27 x 60 = 1,620) + (55 x 24 = 1,320)

1,620 + 1,320 = 2,940

13,122,000 ÷ 2,940 = 4,463 lbs tension

• •

Tension on Sling "B":
(Load × D1 × SB) ÷ [(D2 × H1) + (D1 × H2)]

(Load × D1 × SB)
6000 x 55 x 30 = 9,900,000

(D2 × H1)   +   (D1 × H2)
27 x 60 = 1,620   55 x 24 = 1,320
1,620 + 1,320 = 2,940

9,900,000 ÷ 2,940 = 3,367 lbs tension

> *NOTE: Irregular shaped and distributed loads
> can create unexpected stresses. Consider using
> a minimum 6:1 safety factor for these situations.*

MATH

EXAMPLES

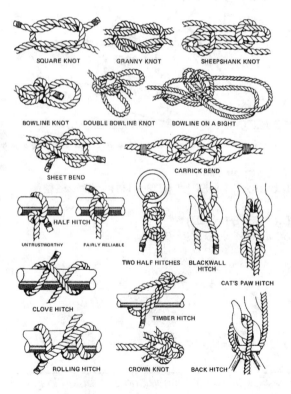

SQUARE KNOT   GRANNY KNOT   SHEEPSHANK KNOT

BOWLINE KNOT   DOUBLE BOWLINE KNOT   BOWLINE ON A BIGHT

SHEET BEND   CARRICK BEND

HALF HITCH

UNTRUSTWORTHY   FAIRLY RELIABLE

TWO HALF HITCHES   BLACKWALL HITCH

CAT'S PAW HITCH

CLOVE HITCH   TIMBER HITCH

ROLLING HITCH   CROWN KNOT   BACK HITCH

Basket Hitches

There is a great misconception about what is a "true" basket hitch. A true basket hitch is one in which a wire rope sling is in contact with a round surface that has a diameter of 20 or more times the rope diameter. Also note that the slings angle MUST be within 5 degrees of vertical to achieve this "true" basket rating.

5° max

When D is 20 times the component rope diameter (d) D the D/d Ratio is expressed as 20/1.

A sling wrapped around a rectangular surface is NOT a true basket unless the corners have a radius equal to the D/d shown in the above illustration. With a flat synthetic web sling, the capacity of the sling would have to be cross referenced to an equivalent strength wire rope, and the load diameter equal to 20 wire rope diameters.

EXAMPLES

CAUTION: A wire rope attached to an object of equal diameter, such as another wire rope or a small shackle, will have a strength rating of 50%. Small diameters have a shearing effect on the slings when used like this.

Shackle examples

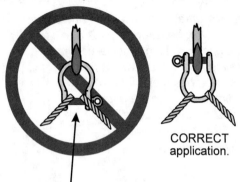

CORRECT
application.

INCORRECT!
The shackle pin is in tension,
and could result in failure.

Use washers to shim
excess space between
shackle and hook.

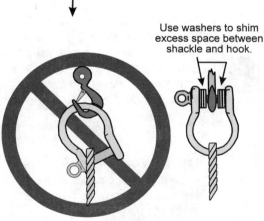

Shackles are designed to be used with "in-line" forces to take advantage of the shear design of the pin and shackle body.

Wire rope, pin/hook diameters

ANSI B30.9* qualifies the contact surface between a portion of the sling and the load or shackle as "a contact surface which shall have a diameter of curvature at least double the diameter of the rope from which the sling is made". This standard specifically addresses natural and synthetic fiber rope, but many local codes and standards apply this rule to wire rope also. Check with local authorities to determine how it applies in your specific area. Regardless of legal jurisdiction, it is considered a good practice to apply this standard to all forms of slings used with lifting and hoisting operations to maximize the safe working limits of the equipment, and minimize the chance for premature failure.

The contact surface of the shackle should have a MINIMUM diameter of at least twice the diameter of the sling being used.

EXAMPLES

*Extracted from American National Standard Slings, ANSI B30.9, used with permission of the publisher.

Synthetic slings, pin/hook diameter

Recommended MINIMUM shackle and pin sizes for Roundslings		
Color	**Shackle Diameters (inches)**	
	Stock	**Pin**
Purple	1/2"	1/2"
Green	3/4"	3/4"
Yellow	3/4"	3/4"
Tan	7/8"	1"
Red	1"	1-1/8"
Orange	1"	1-1/8"
Blue	1-1/4"	1-3/8"
Grey	1-1/2"	1-5/8"
Brown	1-3/4"	2"

RDSL-PIN.TBL

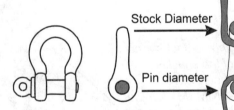

Stock Diameter

Pin diameter

Using a smaller diameter than those listed will reduce the S.W.L. of the sling.

These values are typical, always consult the manufacturer of the sling for the exact data for the make of sling being used.

Thimbles and sliding choker hooks

The use of thimbles in wire rope eyes are an excellent way to minimize damage caused from incorrect pin/ hook sizing.

When using wire rope slings in a choker hitch, the eye must never be used in direct contact with the sling body. This will cause a reduction in S.W.L. by as much as 50%. Using a thimble eye may reduce this problem, but a large shackle or a sliding choker hook is the best way to choke with wire rope.

A sliding hook choker is superior to a shackle or unprotected eye, since it provides a greater bending radius for the sling body.

EXAMPLES

Choker hitch usage.

Web slings should not be "choked" back on the eye or at the base of the eye. This can cause damage to the fibers, and will reduce the S.W.L. of the sling.

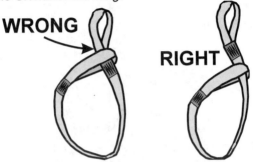

When placing a single flat web synthetic sling over a hook, never force the eye over the hook (as shown in the lower right) the eye should fit without increasing the vertical angles of the legs formed by the eye.

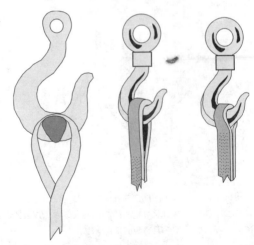

Sling limitations & precautions

*Nylon web slings shall not be used where fumes, vapors, sprays, mists or liquids of **acids** or phenolics are present.*

*Polyester and polypropylene web slings shall not be used where fumes, vapors, sprays, mists or liquids of **caustics** are present.*

*Synthetic web slings made of polyester or **nylon** fibers shall not be used above **180 deg. F.***

*Polypropylene web slings shall not be used above of **200 deg. F.***

Fiber core** wire rope slings of all grades shall be permanently removed from service if they are exposed to temperatures in excess of **200 deg. F.

*If nonfiber core wire rope slings (**IWRC**) of any grades are used at temperatures above **400** deg. F or below **minus 60** deg. F, the specific recommendations of the sling manufacturer regarding use at that temperature shall be followed.*

The rules listed on this page were taken from the OSHA standard, 29 CFR 1910.184

EXAMPLES

Choker hitch Rated capacity adjustment	
Angle of choke in degrees	**Rated capacity ***
Over 120	100%
90 - 120	87%
60 - 89	74%
30 - 59	62%
0 - 29	49%

CHOK-CAP.TBL

*Values are for I.W.R.C. and fibre core wire rope, the percentage listed is the percentage of sling rated capacity in a choker hitch.

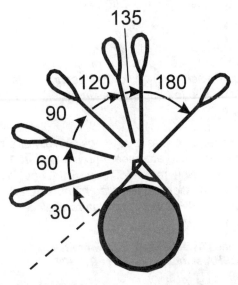

Angle of choke

Choker Hitch configurations affect the rated capacity of a sling. This is because the sling leg or body is passed around the load, through one eye and is suspended by the other eye. The contact of the sling body with the eye causes a loss of sling strength at this point. If a load is hanging free, the normal choke is approximately 135 degrees. When the angle is less than 135 degrees an adjustment in the sling rated capacity must be made, as shown in the table on the facing page.

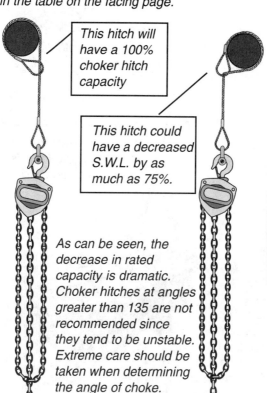

This hitch will have a 100% choker hitch capacity

This hitch could have a decreased S.W.L. by as much as 75%.

As can be seen, the decrease in rated capacity is dramatic. Choker hitches at angles greater than 135 are not recommended since they tend to be unstable. Extreme care should be taken when determining the angle of choke.

Wide web slings vs wire rope

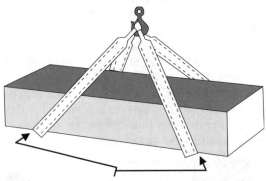

Care must be used when wide synthetic slings are used to avoid tearing and ultimate failure.

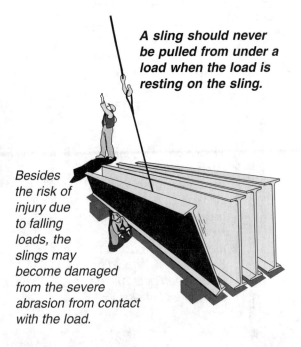

A sling should never be pulled from under a load when the load is resting on the sling.

Besides the risk of injury due to falling loads, the slings may become damaged from the severe abrasion from contact with the load.

Softeners

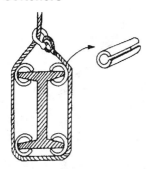

All sharp corners should be covered by pads or softeners to prevent the sling from being bent or cut by the load. These softeners can be made from wooden blocks, or fabricated from steel pipe shapes.

Slings shall not be shortened with knots or bolts or other makeshift devices.

Spreaders and eyebolts

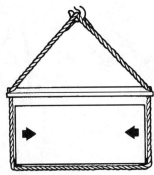

Use a spreader bar between legs of a sling to prevent excessive side pressure on the load by the sling during the lift.

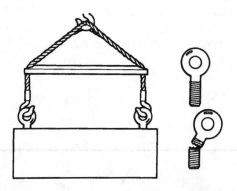

When attaching a sling to eye bolts, always pull in line with the bolt axis. Eye bolts with shoulders may take some angular loading, but shoulderless types (like shown above) will break when angular stress is applied to them.

Side loading hooks

Hooks are designed for in-line tension only.

Hooks, like most rigging components, are designed to have loads applied to them in a straight line pull. Whenever a hook is used in the positions shown at the right, there is an increased chance that it will fail.

The illustration on the bottom shows a hook that is being "tip loaded". This is not recommended with standard hooks, although special hooks called sorting hooks are designed for this type of application.

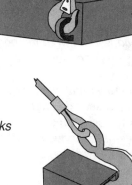

EXAMPLES

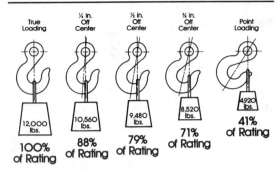

True Loading	¼ in. Off Center	½ in. Off Center	¾ in. Off Center	Point Loading
12,000 lbs.	10,560 lbs.	9,480 lbs.	8,520 lbs.	4920 lbs.
100% of Rating	88% of Rating	79% of Rating	71% of Rating	41% of Rating

Hooks are designed to carry the load in-line or in a "true loading" position. The Safe Working Load ratings are based on this assumption. As shown above, the SWL decreases rapidly when the load is moved off center.

Based on the same theory, when multiple slings are placed on a hook the rating will also be decreased (as shown on the right). This is because the tension on the hook is trying to open it up, or spread it apart. This is obviously not what the hook was designed for.

Whenever multiple slings are used, a shackle should always be used to prevent the reduction of the Safe Working Load ratings of the hook.

Reeving eyebolts

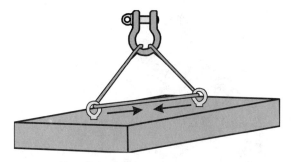

The illustration above shows an extremely POOR rigging practice. By running or "reeving" a single sling through the eye bolts and connecting them to the shackle will dramatically increase the side loading on the eye bolts.

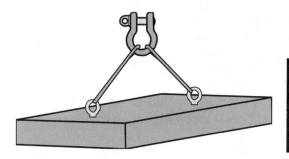

Using two slings will reduce the side loading of the eye bolts as shown in the illustration above, but care must still be taken on the sling angles and the amount of SWL reduction on the eye bolts. Refer to pages 30 - 32 for additional information on eyebolts.

EXAMPLES

Eyebolt applications

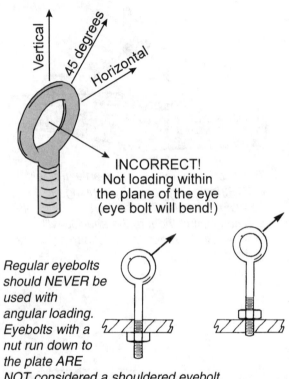

INCORRECT!
Not loading within
the plane of the eye
(eye bolt will bend!)

Regular eyebolts should NEVER be used with angular loading. Eyebolts with a nut run down to the plate ARE NOT considered a shouldered eyebolt, and should not be used at an angle

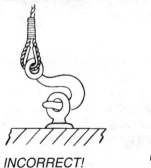

INCORRECT!

CORRECT! Always use a shackle.

GENERAL INFORMATION

General Safety Rules

Safe operating practices.
Whenever any sling is used, the following practices shall be observed:

(1) Slings that are damaged or defective shall not be used.
(2) Slings shall not be shortened with knots or bolts or other makeshift devices.
(3) Sling legs shall not be kinked.
(4) Slings shall not be loaded in excess of their rated capacities.
(5) Slings used in a basket hitch shall have the loads balanced to prevent slippage.
(6) Slings shall be securely attached to their loads.
(7) Slings shall be padded or protected from the sharp edges of their loads.
(8) Suspended loads shall be kept clear of all obstructions.
(9) All employees shall be kept clear of loads about to be lifted and of suspended loads.
(10) Hands or fingers shall not be placed between the sling and its load while the sling is being tightened around the load.
(11) Shock loading is prohibited.
(12) A sling shall not be pulled from under a load when the load is resting on the sling.

GENERAL INFO

Inspections.

Each day before being used, the sling and all
fastenings and attachments shall be
inspected for damage or defects by a
competent person designated by the
employer. Additional inspections shall
be performed during sling use, where
service conditions warrant. Damaged
or defective slings shall be immediately removed from service.

SPECIFIC SLING TOPICS

Alloy steel chain slings.

(1)   Sling identification. Alloy steel chain
slings shall have permanently affixed
durable identification stating size,
grade, rated capacity, and reach.

(2)   Makeshift links or fasteners formed
from bolts or rods, or other such
attachments, shall not be used.

(3)   A thorough periodic inspection of alloy
steel chain slings in use shall be made
on a regular basis, to be determined
on the basis of (A) frequency of sling
use; (B) severity of service conditions;
(C) nature of lifts being made; and (D)
experience gained on the service life
of slings used in similar circum-
stances. Such inspections shall in no
event be at intervals greater than once
every 12 months.

(4)   The employer shall make and maintain a record of the most recent month
in which each alloy steel chain sling
was thoroughly inspected, and shall

make such record available for examination.   1910.184(e)(3)(ii)

(5)   The thorough inspection of alloy steel chain slings shall be performed by a competent person designated by the employer, and shall include a thorough inspection for wear, defective welds, deformation and increase in length. Where such defects or deterioration are present, the sling shall be immediately removed from service.

(6)   Safe operating temperatures. Alloy steel chain slings shall be permanently removed from service if they are heated above 1000 deg. F. When exposed to service temperatures in excess of 600 deg. F, the maximum working load limits shall be reduced in accordance with the chain or sling manufacturer's recommendations.

(7)   Slings shall be removed from service if hooks are cracked, have been opened more than 15 percent of the normal throat opening measured at the narrowest point or twisted more than 10 degrees from the plane of the unbent hook.

Wire rope slings.

(1)   Wire rope slings shall not be used with loads in excess of the rated capacities shown in the current OSHA/ANSI standards (also shown in this edition of the "Rigging Handbook").

(2)   Slings not included in these tables shall be used only in accordance with the manufacturer's recommendations.

GENERAL INFO

(3)   Safe operating temperatures. Fiber core wire rope slings of all grades shall be permanently removed from service if they are exposed to temperatures in excess of 200 deg. F. When nonfiber core wire rope slings of any grade are used at temperatures above 400 deg. F or below minus 60 deg. F, recommendations of the sling manufacturer regarding use at that temperature shall be followed.

(4)   Wire rope slings shall be immediately removed from service if any of the following conditions are present:

(i) Ten randomly distributed broken wires in one rope lay, or five broken wires in one strand in one rope lay.

(ii) Wear or scraping of one-third the original diameter of outside individual wires.

(iii) Kinking, crushing, bird caging or any other damage resulting in distortion of the wire rope structure.

(iv) Evidence of heat damage.

(v) End attachments that are cracked, deformed or worn.

(vi) Hooks that have been opened more than 15 percent of the normal throat opening measured at the narrowest point or twisted more than 10 degrees from the plane of the unbent hook.

(vii) Corrosion of the rope or end attachments.

Metal mesh slings

(1)   Each metal mesh sling shall have permanently affixed to it a durable marking that states the rated capacity for vertical basket hitch and choker hitch loadings.

(2)   Handles. Handles shall have a rated capacity at least equal to the metal fabric and exhibit no deformation after proof testing.

(3)   Attachments of handles to fabric. The fabric and handles shall be joined so that:
(i) The rated capacity of the sling is not reduced.
(ii) The load is evenly distributed across the width of the fabric.
(iii) Sharp edges will not damage the fabric.

(4)   Metal mesh slings which are not impregnated with elastomers may be used in a temperature range from minus 20 deg. F to plus 550 deg. F without decreasing the working load limit. Metal mesh slings impregnated with polyvinyl chloride or neoprene may be used only in a temperature range from zero degrees to plus 200 deg. F. For operations outside these temperature ranges or for metal mesh slings impregnated with other materials, the sling manufacturer's recommendations shall be followed.

(5)   Metal mesh slings shall be immedi-

ately removed from service if any of
the following conditions are present:
(i) A broken weld or broken brazed
joint along the sling edge.
(ii) Reduction in wire diameter of 25
per cent due to abrasion or 15 per
cent due to corrosion.
(iii) Lack of flexibility due to distortion
of the fabric.
(iv) Distortion of the female handle so
that the depth of the slot is increased
more than 10 per cent.
(v) Distortion of either handle so that
the width of the eye is decreased
more than 10 per cent.
(vi) A 15 percent reduction of the
original cross sectional area of metal
at any point around the handle eye.
(vii) Distortion of either handle out of
its plane.

Synthetic web slings
(1)   Sling identification. Each sling shall be
        marked or coded to show the rated
        capacities for each type of hitch and
        type of synthetic web material.
(2)   When synthetic web slings are used,
        the following precautions shall be
        taken:
        (i) Nylon web slings shall not be used
        where fumes, vapors, sprays, mists or
        liquids of acids or phenolics are
        present.

(ii) Polyester and polypropylene web slings shall not be used where fumes, vapors, sprays, mists or liquids of caustics are present.

(iii) Web slings with aluminum fittings shall not be used where fumes, vapors, sprays, mists or liquids of caustics are present.

(3) Synthetic web slings of polyester and nylon shall not be used at temperatures in excess of 180 deg. F.

(4) Polypropylene web slings shall not be used at temperatures in excess of 200 deg. F.

(5) Synthetic web slings shall be immediately removed from service if any of the following conditions are present:

(i) Acid or caustic burns;

(ii) Melting or charring of any part of the sling surface;

(iii) Snags, punctures, tears or cuts;

(iv) Broken or worn stitches; or

(v) Distortion of fittings.

Chainfalls & Come-a-longs

(1) Inspected prior to use.

(2) The hoist chain shall not be wrapped around the load being lifted.

(3) Only qualified individuals shall perform maintenance or repairs on this equipment.

Lifting Beams

(1)   Must have permanent markings affixed and displayed with the follwing:
    (i) Manufacturer's name and address
    (ii) Serial Number
    (iii) Weight of lifting device, if over 100 lbs.
    (iv) Rated load.

(2)   Design factor of at least 3.

(3)   All welding in accordance with ANSI/ AWS D1.1

(4)   Periodic inspections for structural deficiencies.

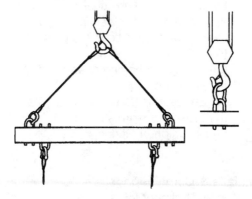

These rules were based on 29 CFR 1910.184 (OSHA), ASME/ANSI B30.20, ASME/ANSI B30.10, and ANSI/ASME B30.9, some areas were paraphrased for brevity and clarity.

Local, state, or site specific regulations may supersede these. Consult local compentent engineering sources for clarification.

Schedule 40 pipe data

Nominal	OD	ID	Weight per foot
1/2"	0.840	0.622	0.851
3/4"	1.050	0.824	1.131
1"	1.315	1.049	1.679
1-1/4"	1.660	1.380	2.273
1-1/2"	1.900	1.610	2.718
2"	2.375	2.067	3.653
2-1/2"	2.875	2.469	5.793
3"	3.500	3.068	7.576
3-1/2"	4.000	3.548	9.109
4"	4.500	4.026	10.79
4-1/2"	5.000	4.506	12.53
5"	5.563	5.047	14.62
6"	6.625	6.065	18.970
8"	8.625	7.981	28.550
10"	10.750	10.020	40.480
12"	12.750	11.938	49.560
14"	14.000	13.124	63.440
16"	16.000	15.000	82.770

PIPE40.TBL

Schedule 80 pipe data

Nominal	OD	ID	Weight per foot
1/2"	0.840	0.546	1.09
3/4"	1.050	0.742	1.47
1"	1.315	0.957	2.17
1-1/4"	1.660	1.278	3.00
1-1/2"	1.900	1.500	3.63
2"	2.375	1.939	5.02
2-1/2"	2.875	2.323	7.66
3"	3.500	2.900	10.25
3-1/2"	4.000	3.364	12.50
4"	4.500	3.826	14.98
4-1/2"	5.000	4.290	17.61
5"	5.563	4.813	20.78
6"	6.625	5.761	28.57
8"	8.625	7.625	43.39
10"	10.750	9.750	64.43
12"	12.750	11.376	88.63
14"	14.000	12.500	106.13
16"	16.000	15.000	82.770

PIPE80.TBL

Weight of steel round stock

Diameter	Weight per foot
1/2"	0.668
3/4"	1.502
1"	2.670
1-1/4"	4.173
1-1/2"	6.008
2"	10.680
2-1/2"	16.690
3"	24.03
3-1/2"	32.710
4"	42.730
4-1/2"	54.080
5"	66.760
6"	96.130
7"	130.800
8"	170.900
9"	216.300
10"	267.000

ROUND.TBL

Weight of steel sheets

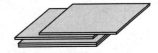

Thickness	lbs. per sq. ft.
3/16"	7.66
1/4"	10.21
5/16"	12.76
3/8"	15.32
7/16"	17.87
1/2"	20.42
9/16"	22.97
5/8"	25.53
11/16"	28.08
3/4"	30.63
7/8"	35.74
1"	40.84
2"	81.68
3"	122.52
4"	163.36
5"	204.2
6"	245.04
7"	285.88
8"	326.72

SHEETS.TBL

Weight of steel strips

Width	Thickness			
	Weight per foot			
	1/4"	3/8"	1/2"	3/4"
1"	0.85	1.28	1.70	2.55
2"	1.70	2.55	3.40	5.10
3"	2.55	3.83	5.10	7.65
4"	3.40	5.10	6.80	10.20
5"	4.25	6.38	8.50	12.75
6"	5.10	7.65	10.20	15.30
7"	5.95	8.93	11.90	17.85
8"	6.80	10.20	13.60	20.40

FLATS.TBL

GENERAL
INFO

Safe loads on timber beams
Load concentrated at center of span

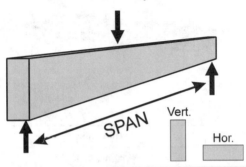

	Span, in feet						
	4	6	8	10	12	14	16
SIZE	Safe Load in lbs.						
4 x 4	990	650	480	380	310	260	220
4 x 6 Hor.	1530	1010	750	590	480	400	340
6 x 6	3440	2290	1700	1340	1110	930	800
6 x 8 Hoz.	4700	3120	2320	1830	1510	1270	1090
6 x 8 Vert.	6430	4260	3180	2520	2080	1760	1520
8 x 8	6690	6660	4330	3440	2840	2400	2070
10 x 10	10740	10690	10640	7020	5800	4930	4270
12 x 12	15690	15620	15550	12490	10340	8790	7630
14 x 14	21630	21520	21420	21320	16780	14290	12410

TIMBEAM.TBL

Safe loads on timber columns

LOAD

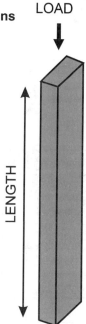

These charts are based on yellow pine of fir timber in first class condition. Weight transfer is based on the post bearing surface distribuded over a greater area of yellow pine or other suitable material. Dimensions are for rough lumber, not surfaced.

LENGTH

	Length, in feet						
	8	10	12	14	16	18	20
SIZE	Safe Load in TONS						
4 x 4	4.7	3.9					
6 x 6	13.4	12.2	10.9	9.8	8.6	7.5	6.3
8 x 8	27.3	25.6	23.9	22.4	20.8	19.2	17.5
10 x 10	45.9	43.9	41.9	39.8	37.7	35.7	33.6
12 x 12	69.4	66.9	64.5	61.9	59.4	56.9	54.5
14 x 14	97.7	94.8	91.8	88.9	85.9	83.1	80.2

TIMPOST.TBL

GENERAL INFO

Decimal Equivelents

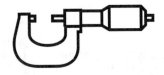

Fraction	Decimal	Fraction	Decimal
1/32"	0.031	17/32"	0.531
1/16"	0.063	9/16"	0.563
3/32"	0.094	19/32"	0.594
1/8"	0.125	5/8"	0.625
5/32"	0.156	21/32"	0.656
3/16"	0.188	11/16"	0.688
7/32"	0.219	23/32"	0.719
1/4"	0.250	3/4"	0.750
9/32"	0.281	25/32"	0.781
5/16"	0.313	13/16"	0.813
11/32"	0.344	27/32"	0.844
3/8"	0.375	7/8"	0.875
13/32"	0.406	29/32"	0.906
7/16"	0.438	15/16"	0.938
15/32"	0.469	31/32"	0.969
1/2"	0.500	1"	1.000

FRACDEC.TBL

Hand signals

Use Main Hoist. Tap fist on head, then use regular signals.

Use Whipline (Auxiliary Hoist) Tap elbow with one hand, then use regular signals.

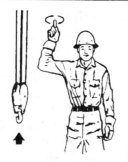

Hoist. With forearm vertical, forefinger pointing up, move hand in small horizontal circle.

Lower. With arm extended downward, forefinger pointing down, move hand in small horizontal circles.

Raise Boom. Arm extended, fingers closed, thumb pointing upward.

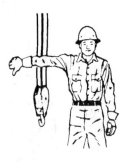

Lower Boom. Arm extended, fingers closed, thumb pointing downward.

Raise the Boom and Lower the Load. With arm extended, thumb pointing up, flex fingers in and out as long as load movement is desired.

Lower the Boom and Raise the Load. With arm extended, thumb pointing down, flex fingers in and out as long as load movement is desired.

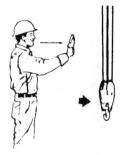

Travel. Arm extended forward, hand open and slightly raised, make pushing motion in direction of travel.

Swing. Arm extended, point with finger in direction of swing of boom.

Travel. (One Track) Lock the track on side indicated by raised fist. Travel opposite track in direction indicated by circular motion of other fist, rotated vertically in front of body. (For crawler cranes only)

Travel. (Both Tracks) Use both fists in front of body, making a circular motion about each other, indicating direction of travel, forward or backward. (For crawler cranes only.)

Extend Boom (Telescoping Booms). Both fists in front of body with thumbs pointing outward.

Retract Boom (Telescoping Booms). Both fists in front of body with thumbs pointing toward each other.

Extend Boom (Telescoping Boom). One Hand Signal. One fist in front of chest with thumb tapping chest.

Retract Boom (Telescoping Boom). One Hand Signal. One fist in front of chest, thumb pointing outward and heel of fist tapping chest.

Stop. Arm extended, palm down, hold position rigidly.

Emergency Stop. Arm extended, palm down, move hand rapidly right and left.

Move Slowly. Use one hand to give any motion signal and place other hand motionless in front of hand giving the motion signal. (Hoist slowly shown as example.)

Dog Everything. Clasp hands in front of body.

GENERAL INFO

Additional Signals for Bridge Cranes

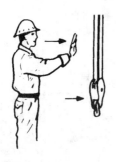

Bridge Travel. Arm extended forward, hand open and slightly raised, make pushing motion in direction of travel.

Trolley Travel. Palm up, fingers closed, thumb pointing in direction of motion, jerk hand horizontally.

Multiple Trolleys. Hold up one finger for block marked "1" and two fingers for block marked "2". Regular signals follow.

Magnet is Disconnected. Crane Operator spreads both hands apart palms up.

Hand signals, courtesy of the Wire Rope Technical Board.

NOTES

NOTES

NOTES

For additional copies of this handbook or other technical training needs please contact:

ACRA Enterprises
2769 W. Glenlord Rd.
Stevensville, MI 49127
Phone (616) 429-6240
FAX (616) 429-1043